baltics

östersjöar

SELECTED WORKS BY TOMAS TRANSTRÖMER IN ENGLISH

20 Poems (Robert Bly, trans.)

Night Vision (Robert Bly, trans.)

Windows & Stones (May Swenson, trans.)

Baltics (Samuel Charters, trans.)

Truth Barriers (Robert Bly, trans.)

Selected Poems 1954-1986 (Robert Hass, ed.)

The Half-Finished Heaven (Robert Bly, trans.)

The Great Enigma (Robin Fulton, trans.)

The Deleted World (Robin Robertson, trans.)

The Sorrow Gondola (Michael McGriff and Mikaela Grassl, trans.)

Tomas Tranströmer's First Poems and Notes from the Land of Lap Fever
(Malena Mörling, trans.)

Prison: Nine Haiku from Hällby Youth Prison (1959)
(Malena Mörling, trans.)

Inspired Notes (John F. Deane, trans.)

Memories Look at Me (Robin Fulton, trans.)

For the Living and the Dead (John F. Deane, trans.)

baltics

östersjöar

TOMAS TRANSTRÖMER

translated by **SAMUEL CHARTERS**
photographs by **ANN CHARTERS**

TAVERN BOOKS

Portland & Salt Lake City

Printed in the United States of America.

Cover art: Cecilia Yang, *Sextant*, 2011. Ink drawing.
Copyright © Cecilia Yang. Courtesy of the artist.

Author photo: Paula Tranströmer.
Copyright © Paula Tranströmer. Courtesy of the artist.

The Swedish text first appeared in *Östersjöar*, Bonniers, 1974, and is reprinted here by permission of the author.

This translation first appeared in *Baltics*, Oyez, 1975. Additional translations by Samuel Charters.

Tranströmer, Tomas, 1931-
Charters, Samuel, 1929-
Charters, Ann, 1936-

ISBN-13: 978-1-935635-14-7
ISBN-10: 1-9356-3514-X

FIRST EDITION

98765432 First Printing

TAVERN BOOKS
Portland & Salt Lake City
www.tavernbooks.com

CONTENTS

Tomas Tranströmer has always been impatient with any effort to make the poet more important than the poem he's written, and he's never been interested in the kind of personality nimbus that drifts, like a small rainbow, over the careers of many popular poets in England and America. But an introduction does seem necessary for someone who isn't familiar with the Swedish literary scene—especially to set the new long poem in its place in his work.

Tomas was born in 1931 and lived for much of his early life in the section of Stockholm known as Södermalm—a large island south of the oldest section of the city with an individual character that makes it, for Swedes, something like Brooklyn used to be for Americans. His poems began appearing in literary magazines while he was still a student, and his first book, *17 Poems*, was published in 1954, when he was twenty-three. The critical response to it was interested but guarded. The word most used was "promising," but other poets recognized that his poetry was considerably more than promising, and the book was an immediate success.

His second book, *Secrets Along the Way*, was published four years later, and like the first book it was small, only fourteen poems and most of them short. In part it was because he'd been traveling—Iceland, Africa, the Balkans, among other places—but also because this was his way of working. His books were small, but they never had the sense of being slight or half finished. They were complete and self sustained, and there was never the feeling of a wasted word or phrase. Each book was what he wanted it to be, and each of them clearly compressed within its tight limits a large mass of emotional and psychological material, even if what he left visible was only the image that clarified the whole. Most poets publish too much—poems that are only suggestions, poems that are filled out with tentative or even vaguer language—but each of his poems seemed to take a definitive place in the larger pattern of the books. At the same time one of the most startling things about the poems was that each of them, despite the effort of compression and distillation that had gone into them, still kept a loose—almost free—spontaneity, as though he'd jotted them down on bits of paper as he drove to work through the Swedish winter darkness.

Through the sixties the books continued to come out at four-year intervals. *The Half-Finished Sky* appeared in 1962, and *Night Vision* in 1970. Unlike most European poets, who have careers as journalists or reviewers, he did no other writing. By the third and fourth books he was recognized as one of Sweden's most significant poets, but he stayed outside the mainstream of Swedish literary life. For many years he was a prison psychologist, even though he now spends more time writing. He and his wife and their two daughters live in a row house in a new development in a small city about sixty miles west of Stockholm and he comes in as seldom as possible.

In the 1970s Tomas broke the four-year pattern he'd set with his earlier books. In 1973 he published a book called *Paths*, which for the first time included a lengthy group of translations. Eleven of the poems were his own, five were translations of the work of close friends, the American poet Robert Bly, and eight were translations of the Hungarian poet János Pilinszky. It was a completely realized book, but at the same time it seemed to be looking to something else. The something else was *Baltics*, which he'd been working on for some years, and which was published with great success in the fall of 1974.

Baltics was in many ways a change of ground for him. Unlike the earlier books it was a single long poem, and it was more personal, almost conversational, in a way he hadn't written before. A number of things went into the composition of the poem, one of them his visit to Latvia and Estonia on the Baltic's eastern shore and his experience of the Baltic as a frontier and at the same time a route of communication.

Two poems in *Night Vision* in 1970 also suggested one of the changes in his life that moved him to write the new poem. In one of three "Preludes" he suddenly said,

> The apartment where I lived for more than half of
> my life had to be vacated. It's been emptied now of
> everything...

and in the last poem of the book he described a bookcase.

> It was brought from the apartment of the person
> who had died. It stood empty a few days, empty, before
> I filled it with books...

What had touched him so deeply was the death of his mother after a long illness. As he described it in the poem, in an image growing out of his hospital visits, "The death lectures went on for several terms..." Of *Baltics* itself he wrote,

I looked at the sky and the earth and straight ahead
and since then I've been writing a long letter to the
    dead
on a typewriter that doesn't have a ribbon, only a
    horizon line
so words beat in vain and nothing stays...

The poem is largely about his family and the island in the archipelago off the east coast of Sweden where they lived for many years, and where he returns each summer with his wife and children. The poem is in some ways almost like taking a summer walk with Tomas across the island's stretches of forest and overgrown fields. Sometimes—along open stretches of path or along the dirt roads—he walks hurriedly, but in the forests he walks slowly and thoughtfully, stopping to look for mushrooms or wildflowers. With each cluster of mushrooms, or single swelling shape in the shadows, he bends down to taste and smell them—breaking them open with practiced fingers to see if he or the worms has gotten to them first. As he strides ahead of you he talks—about the island, about his family and their life on it— and it's these things he talks about that became the poem *Baltics*.

SAMUEL CHARTERS
Saltsjö Boo

TRANSLATOR'S NOTE TO THE 1975 EDITION

There are two words in Swedish to describe a rendering of a poem from one language into another. One is *översättning*, which means "translation," and the other is *tolkning*, which is close to the English word "version." In English the distinction is often blurred, and there is particularly a tendency to describe unrhymed renderings of rhymed poetry as translations, when they are actually versions. In Swedish, however, the distinctions are considered important, and this is an *översättning*: a translation. With some poems a great deal of the original can be lost in a translation, but with a poem like *Baltics*; unrhymed, rhythmically rather free, and in a contemporary idiom, it is possible to come fairly close to the original; especially since Swedish and English share a large root vocabulary, and there are many points where grammatical forms are similar. What is most obviously different is the sound of the English, which is a softer language with a rounding at the edges from the romance languages that helped form it. Swedish has a harder sound, more abrupt, and this tone is difficult to bring across.

As with most Swedish writers, English is a second language for Tomas, and we worked closely together on every aspect of the translation. At troublesome points he was often the best judge of how well the Swedish and the English reflected each other. Also he and his family made my family welcome on the island off the Swedish coast that figures so often in the poem, and the long summer days with them there gave me a feeling of the poem I couldn't have gotten in any other way. In a very immediate sense, if we were trying to decide if the translation of a word should be something like either "bay" or "channel" we walked down to the shore to look at what he was describing. We worked out as many problems on afternoon walks as we did at the kitchen table in the evenings with notes and dictionaries.

Most of the references in the poem will be clear to anyone with a rudimentary knowledge of the geography of the Baltic, but there are some names that perhaps need more clarification. Tomas has identified Furusund and Sandhamn as pilot stations on the coast, and Leipāja (Libau) is a port in Latvia—now a part of the Soviet Union. Robben Island is a maximum security prison off the African coast where the South African Republic detains political prisoners.

I must thank Professor William McMunn, of the University of Connecticut, for his assistance in translating the 14th century verse chronicle quoted in section V, and I must also thank poet Gunnar Harding, who went over early versions of most of the sections and helped with many points of language and grammar. The translation couldn't have been done without his and Tomas Tranströmer's patient help.

SAMUEL CHARTERS
Saltsjö Boo

baltics

östersjöar

I

Det var före radiomasternas tid.

Morfar var nybliven lots. I almanackan skrev han upp de fartyg
han lotsade—
namn, destinationer, djupgång.

Exempel från 1884:
Ångf Tiger Capt Rowan 16 fot Hull Gefle Furusund
Brigg Ocean Capt Andersen 8 fot Sandöfjord Hernösand
Furusund
Ångf St Pettersburg Capt Libenberg 11 fot Stettin Libau
Sandhamn

Han tog ut dem till Östersjön, genom den underbara labyrinten
av öar och vatten.
Och de som möttes ombord och bars av samma skrov några
timmar eller dygn,
hur mycket lärde de känna varann?
Samtal på felstavad engelska, samförstånd och missförstånd men
mycket lite av medveten lögn.
Hur mycket lärde de känna varann?

När det var tät tjocka: halv fart, knappt ledsyn. Ur det osynliga
kom udden med ett enda kliv och var alldeles intill.
Brölande signal varannan minut. Ögonen läste rätt in i det
osynliga.

It was before the time of radio masts.

My grandfather was a newly licensed pilot. In the almanac he
    wrote down the vessels he piloted—
name, destination, draft:
Examples from 1884:
Steamer Tiger   Capt Rowan   16 feet   Gefle Furusund
Brig Ocean   Capt Andersen   8 feet   Sandöfjord Hernösand
    Furusund
Steamer St Petersburg   Capt Libenberg   11 feet   Stettin Libau
    Sandhamn

He took them out to the Baltic, through that wonderful labyrinth
    of islands and water.
And those that met on board, and were carried by the same hull
    for a few hours or a few days,
how well did they get to know each other?
Talking in misspelled English, understanding and misunderstanding,
    but very little conscious lying.
How well did they get to know each other?

When it was thick fog: half speed, almost blind. The headland
    coming out of the invisibility with a single stride, it was right
    on them.
Fog horn blasting every other minute. His eyes reading straight
    into the invisible.

(Hade han labyrinten i huvudet?)
Minuterna gick.
Grund och kobbar memorerade som psalmverser.

Och den där känslan av "just här är vi" som måste hållas kvar, som
när man bär på ett bräddfullt kärl och ingenting får spillas.

En blick ner i maskinrummet.

Compoundmaskinen, långlivad som ett människohjärta, arbetade
med stora mjukt studsande rörelser, akrobater av stål, och
dofterna steg som från ett kök.

.

.

(Did he have the labyrinth in his head?)
The minutes went by.
Lands and reefs memorized like hymn verses.
And the feeling of we're-right-here that you have to keep, like
carrying a pail filled to the brim without spilling a drop.

A glance down into the engine room.
The compound engine, as long-lived as a human heart, worked
with great soft recoiling movements, steel acrobatics, and the
smells rising from it as from a kitchen.

II

Vinden går i tallskogen. Det susar tungt och lätt,
Östersjön susar också mitt inne på ön, långt inne i skogen är man
ute på öppna sjön.
Den gamla kvinnan hatade suset i träden. Hennes ansikte
stelnade i melankoli när det blåste upp:
"Man måste tänka på dem som är ute i båtarna".
Men hon hörde också något annat i suset, precis som jag, vi är
släkt.
(Vi går tillsammans. Hon är död sen tretti år.)
Det susar ja och nej, missförstånd och samförstånd.
Det susar tre barn friska, ett på sanatorium och två döda.
Det stora draget som blåser liv i somliga lågor och blåser ut andra.
Villkoren.
Det susar: Fräls mig Herre, vattnen tränger mig inpå livet.
Man går länge och lyssnar och når då en punkt där gränserna
öppnas
eller snarare
där allting blir gräns. En öppen plats försänkt i mörker.
Människorna strömmar ut från de svagt upplysta
byggnaderna runt om. Det sorlar.

Ett nytt vinddrag och platsen ligger åter öde och tyst.

Ett nytt vinddrag, det brusar om andra stränder.
Det handlar om kriget.
Det handlar om platser där medborgarna är under kontroll,

The wind walks in the pine forest. It sighs heavily, lightly.
In the middle of the forest the Baltic also sighs, deep in the forest
　　you're out on the open sea.
The old woman hated the sighing in the trees, her face hardened
　　in melancholy when the wind rose:
"You have to think of those out there in the boats."
But she also heard something else in the sighing, as I do, we're
　　related.
(We're walking together. She's been dead for thirty years.)
It sighs yes and no, understanding and misunderstanding.
It sighs three children healthy, one in the sanitarium and two dead.
The broad current that blows some flames into life and blows
　　others out. Conditions.
It sighs: Save me, Lord, the waters are come unto my soul.
You walk around listening for a long time, finally reaching the
　　point where the boundaries begin to open out
or rather
where everything becomes boundaries. An open square sunk in
　　darkness. People streaming out of the dimly lit buildings
　　around it. A murmuring.

A new gust of wind and the square again lies solitary and still.

A new gust of wind that sighs of other shores.
It deals with war.
It deals with places where the citizens are controlled,

där tankarna byggs med reservutgångar,
där ett samtal bland vänner verkligen blir ett test på vad vänskap
betyder.
Och när man är tillsammans med dem som man inte känner så
väl. Kontroll. En viss uppriktighet är på sin plats
bara man inte släpper med blicken det där som driver i samtalets
utkant: någonting mörkt, en mörk fläck.
Någonting som kan driva in
och förstöra allt. Släpp det inte med blicken!
Vad ska man likna det vid? En mina?
Nej det vore för handfast. Och nästan för fredligt—för på vår
kust har de flesta berättelser om minor ett lyckligt slut,
skräcken begränsad i tiden.
Som i den här historien från fyrskeppet: "Hösten 1915 sov man
oroligt..." etc. En drivmina siktades
när den drev mot fyrskeppet sakta, den sänktes och hävdes,
ibland skymd av sjöarna, ibland framskymtande som en spion
i en folkmassa.
Besättningen låg i ångest och sköt på den med gevär. Förgäves.
Till sist satte man ut en båt
och gjorde fast en lång lina vid minan och bogserade den varsamt
och länge in till experterna.
Efteråt ställde man upp minans mörka skal i en sandig plantering
som prydnad
tillsammans med skalen av Strombus gigas från Västindien.

24

where thoughts are built with emergency exits,
where a conversation between friends is really a test of what
     friendship means.
And when you're together with somebody you don't know well.
     Control. A certain frankness is alright
if you just don't lose sight of something drifting there on the
     outskirts of the conversation: something dark, a dark stain,
something that can drift in
and destroy everything. Don't lose sight of it!
What can it be compared with? A mine?
No, that would be too solid. And almost too peaceful—since on
     our coast most stories about mines end happily, the terror
     limited to the moment.
As this story from the lightship: "Fall 1915 we were sleeping
     uneasily..." etc. A drifting mine was sighted
as it floated calmly toward the lightship, it was sinking, heaving
     up, at times hidden by the waves, at times glimpsed like a spy
     in the crowd.
The crew lying there in agony, shooting at it with rifles. Without
     success. Finally they put out a boat
and made a long line fast to the mine and towed it carefully and
     slowly in to the experts.
Afterwards they set up the mine's dark shell in a sandy little
     stretch of park as an ornament
along with Strombus Gigas shells from the West Indies.

Och havsblåsten går i de torra tallarna längre bort, den har
    bråttom över kyrkogårdens sand,
förbi stenarna som lutar, lotsarnas namn.

Det torra suset
av stora portar som öppnas och stora portar som stängs.

And the gale makes its way through the dry pines beyond, it
    hurries over the sand of the cemetery,
past the leaning stones, the names of the pilots.
The dry sighing
of large gates opening and large gates closing.

III

I den gotländska kyrkans halvmörka hörn, i en dager av mild
   mögel
står en dopfunt av sandsten—1100-tal—stenhuggarens namn
är kvar, framlysande
som en tandrad i en massgrav:
                    HEGWALDR
                    namnet kvar. Och hans bilder
här och på andra krukors väggar, människomyller, gestalter på väg
   ut ur stenen.
Ögonens kärnor av ondska och godhet spränger där.
Herodes vid bordet: den stekta tuppen flyger upp och gal
   "Christus natus est"—servitören avrättades—
intill föds barnet, under klungor av ansikten värdiga och hjälplösa
   som apungars.
Och de frommas flyende steg
ekande över drakfjälliga avloppstrummors gap.
(Bilderna starkare i minnet än när man ser dem direkt, starkast
när funten snurrar i en långsam mullrande karusell i minnet.)
Ingenstans lä. Överallt risk.
Som det var. Som det är.
Bara därinnanför finns frid, i krukans vatten som ingen ser,
men på ytterväggarna rasar kampen.
Och friden kan komma droppvis, kanske om natten

In the half-dark corner of Gotland church, in the mildewed daylight
stands a sandstone baptismal font—12th Century—the stone
    cutter's name
still there, shining
like a row of teeth in a mass grave:
               HEGWALDR
                    the name still there. And his scenes
here and on the sides of other vessels crowded with people, figures
    on their way out of the stone.
The eyes' kernel of good and evil bursting there.
Herod at the table: the roasted cock flying up and crowing
    "Christus natus est"—the servant executed—
close by the child born, under clumps of faces as worthy and
    helpless as young monkeys.
And the fleeing steps of the pious
drumming over the dragon scales of sewer mouths.
(The scenes stronger in memory than when you stand in front of
    them,
strongest when the font spins like a slow, rumbling carousel in
    the memory.)
Nowhere the lee-side. Everywhere risk.
As it was. As it is.
Only inside there is peace, in the water of the vessel that no one
    sees,
but on the outer walls the struggle rages.
And peace can come drop by drop, perhaps at night

när vi ingenting vet,
eller som när man ligger på dropp i en sal på sjukhuset.

Människor, bestar, ornament.
Det finns inget landskap. Ornament.

Mr B***, min reskamrat, älskvärd, i landsflykt,
frisläppt från Robben Island, säger:
"Jag avundas er. Jag känner inget för naturen.
Men *människor i landskap*, det säger mig något."

Här är människor i landskap.
Ett foto från 1865. Ångslupen ligger vid bryggan i sundet.
Fem figurer. En dam i ljus krinolin, som en bjällra, som en blomma.
Karlarna liknar statister i en allmogepjäs.
Alla är vackra, tveksamma, på väg att suddas ut.
De stiger iland en kort stund. De suddas ut.
Ångslupen av utdöd modell—
en hög skorsten, soltak, smalt skrov—
den är fullkomligt främmande, en UFO som landat.
Allt det andra på fotot är chockerande verkligt:
krusningarna på vattnet,
den andra stranden—
jag kan stryka med handen över de skrovliga berghällarna,
jag kan höra suset i granarna.
Det är nära. Det är

when we don't know anything,
or as when we're taped to a drip in a hospital ward.

People, beasts, ornaments.
There isn't any landscape. Ornaments.

Mr. B***, my traveling companion, amiable, in exile,
escaped from Robben Island, says:
"I envy you. I don't feel anything for nature.
But *figures in landscape*, that says something to me."

Here are figures in landscape.
A photo from 1865. The steamer lies at the dock in the channel.
Five figures. A lady in light crinoline, like a bell, like a flower.
The men are like extras in a folk play.
They're all good-looking, indecisive, beginning to fade out.
They step onshore for a moment. They fade out.
The steamer is an extinct model—
a high funnel, awning, narrow hull—
it's completely strange, a UFO that's landed.
Everything else in the photo is shockingly real:
the ripples on the water,
the opposite beach—
I can stroke the rough rocks with my hand,
I can hear the sighing in the spruce.
It's near. It's

idag.
Vågorna är aktuella.

Nu, hundra år senare. Vågorna kommer in från no man's water
och slår mot stenarna.
Jag går längs stranden. Det är inte som det var att gå längs
    stranden.
Man måste gapa över för mycket, föra många samtal på en gång,
    man har tunna väggar.
Varje ting har fått en ny skugga bakom den vanliga skuggan
och man hör den släpa också när det är alldeles mörkt.

Det är natt.

Det strategiska planetariet vrider sig. Linserna stirrar i mörkret.
Natthimlen är full av siffror, och de matas in
i ett blinkande skåp,
en möbel
där det bor energin hos en gräshoppssvärm som kaläter tunnland
    av Somalias jord på en halvtimma.

Jag vet inte om vi är i begynnelsen eller sista stadiet.
Sammanfattningen kan inte göras, sammanfattningen är omöjlig.
Sammanfattningen är alrunan—

34

today.
The waves are topical.

Now, a hundred years later. The waves come in from no man's
    water
and break against the stones.
I walk along the beach. It isn't like it used to be to walk along the
    beach.
You have to swallow too much, keep too many conversations
    going at the same time, you have thin walls.
Everything's gotten a new shadow behind its ordinary shadow,
and you hear it dragging along even when it's completely dark.

It's night.

The strategic planetarium rotates. The lenses stare into the
    darkness.
The night sky is full of numbers, and they're fed into
a blinking cupboard,
a piece of furniture,
inside it the energy of a grasshopper swarm that devours the acres
    of Somalia in half an hour.

I don't know if we're in the beginning or in the final stage.
No conclusion can be made, no conclusion is possible.
The conclusion is the mandrake—

(se uppslagsboken för vidskepelser:

ALRUNA

undergörande växt

som gav ifrån sig ett så ohyggligt skrik när den slets upp ur jorden

att man föll död ner. Hunden fick göra det...)

(see the encyclopedia of superstitions:

MANDRAKE

miracle-working plant
that gave such a dreadful shriek when it was torn out of the earth
that the person fell dead. A dog had to do it...)

IV

Från läsidan,
närbilder.

Blåstång.   I det klara vattnet lyser tångskogarna, de är unga,
man vill emigrera dit, lägga sig raklång på sin
spegelbild och sjunka till ett visst djup—tången
som håller sig uppe med luftblåsor, som vi håller oss
uppe med idéer.

Hornsimpa.   Fisken som är paddan som ville bli fjäril och lyckas
till en tredjedel, gömmer sig i sjögräset men dras upp
med näten, fasthakad med sina patetiska taggar och
vårtor—när man trasslar loss den ur nätmaskorna
blir händerna skimrande av slem.

Berghällen.   Ute på de solvarma lavarna kilar småkrypen, de
har bråttom som sekundvisare—tallen kastar en
skugga, den vandrar sakta som en timvisare—inne
i mig står tiden stilla, oändligt med tid, den tid
som behövs för att glömma alla språk och uppfinna
perpetuum mobile.

På läsidan kan man höra gräset växa: ett svagt trummande
underifrån, ett svagt dån av miljontals små gaslågor, så är det

From the lee-side,
close-ups.

Bladderwrack.   The forests of bladderwrack shine in the clear
water, they're young, you want to emigrate there,
stretch out on your own reflection and sink down
to such and such a depth—the seaweed holding
itself up with air bladders, as we hold ourselves up
with ideas.

Bullhead.   The fish that's a toad that wanted to be a butterfly
and made it a third of the way, hiding himself in
the seaweed, but pulled up in the net, hooked
fast by his pathetic spikes and warts—when you
untangle him from the mesh of the net your hands
shine with slime.

The rocks.   The small creatures hurry over the sun-warmed
lichens, rushing like second hands—the pine
casts a shadow, it wanders slowly like an hour
hand—inside me time stands still, endless time,
the time it takes to forget all languages and invent
perpetual motion.

On the lee-side you can hear the grass growing, a faint drumming
coming from underneath, a faint roar of millions of small gas

att höra gräset växa.

Och nu: vattenvidden, utan dörrar, den öppna gränsen
som växer sig allt bredare
ju längre man sträcker sig ut.

Det finns dagar då Östersjön är ett stilla oändligt tak.
Dröm då naivt om någonting som kommer krypande på taket
och försöker reda ut flagglinorna,
försöker få upp
trasan—

flaggen som är så gnuggad av blåsten och rökt av skorstenarna och
blekt av solen att den kan vara allas.

Men det är långt till Liepāja.

flames, so it is to hear the grass grow.

And now: the stretch of open water, without doors, the open
    boundaries
that grow broader and broader
the further you stretch out.

There are days when the Baltic is a calm, limitless roof.
Then dream innocently of someone crawling out on the roof to
    try to put the halyards in order,
trying to hoist
the rag—

the flag that's so frayed by the wind and smoked by the funnels
    and bleached by the sun that it could be anybody's.

But it's a long way to Liepāja.

V

30 juli.   Fjärden har blivit excentrisk—idag vimlar maneterna för
första gången på åratal, de pumpar sig fram lugnt och
skonsamt, de hör till samma rederi: AURELIA, de driver
som blommor efter en havsbegravning, tar man upp
dem ur vattnet försvinner all form hos dem, som när en
obeskrivlig sanning lyfts upp ur tystnaden och formuleras
till död gelé, ja de är oöversättliga, de måste stanna i sitt
element.

2 augusti.   Någonting vill bli sagt men orden går inte med på det.
Någonting som inte kan sägas,
afasi,
det finns inga ord men kanske en stil...

Det händer att man vaknar om natten
och kastar ner några ord snabbt
på närmaste papper, på kanten av en tidning
(orden strålar av mening!)
men på morgonen: samma ord säger ingenting längre, klotter,
    felsägningar.
Eller fragment av den stora nattliga stilen som drog förbi?

Musiken kommer till en människa, han är tonsättare, spelas, gör
    karriär, blir chef för konservatoriet.
Konjunkturen vänder, han fördöms av myndigheterna.

July 30. The channel has become eccentric—today it's teeming with
        jellyfish for the first time in years, they pump themselves
        along with calm consideration, they belong to the same
        shipping company: AURELIA, they drift like flowers after
        a burial at sea, if you take them out of the water all of
        their shape disappears, as when an indescribable truth is
        lifted up out of the silence and formulated into a lifeless
        mass, yes, they're untranslatable, they have to stay in their
        element.

August 2. Something wants to be said, but the words don't agree.
Something that can't be said,
aphasia,
there aren't any words but maybe a style...

Sometimes you wake up at night
and quickly throw some words down
on the nearest paper, on the margin of a newspaper
(the words glowing with meaning!)
but in the morning: the same words don't say anything anymore,
        scrawls, misspeakings.
Or fragments of a great nightly style that dragged past?

Music comes to a person, he's a composer, he's played, has a career,
        becomes director of the conservatory.
The trend turns downward, he's blamed by the authorities.

Som huvudåklagare sätter man upp hans elev K***.
Han hotas, degraderas, förpassas.
Efter några år minskar onåden, han återupprättas.
Då kommer hjärnblödningen: högersidig förlamning med afasi,
    kan bara uppfatta korta fraser, säger fel ord.
Kan alltså inte nås av upphöjelse eller fördömanden.
Men musiken finns kvar, han komponerar fortfarande i sin egen
    stil,
han blir en medicinsk sensation den tid han har kvar att leva.

Han skrev musik till texter han inte längre förstod—
på samma sätt
uttrycker vi något med våra liv
i den nynnande kören av felsägningar.

Dödsföreläsningarna pågick flera terminer. Jag var närvarande
tillsammans med kamrater som jag inte kände
(vilka är ni?)
—efteråt gick var och en till sitt, profiler.

Jag såg mot himlen och mot marken och rakt fram
och skriver sen dess ett långt brev till de döda
på en maskin som inte har färgband bara en horisontstrimma
så orden bultar förgäves och ingenting fastnar.

Jag står med handen på dörrhandtaget, tar pulsen på huset.

They put up his pupil K*** as chief prosecutor.
He's threatened, demoted, sent away.
After some years the disgrace diminishes, he's rehabilitated.
Then comes the stroke: right-side paralysis and aphasia, can only
    grasp short phrases, says wrong words.
Can, as a result of this, not be touched by advancement or blame.
But the music's still there, he still composes in his own style,
he becomes a medical sensation for the time he has left to live.

He wrote music to texts he no longer understood—
in the same way
we express something with our lives
in that humming chorus of misspeech.

The Death lectures went on for several terms. I was present
together with classmates I didn't know
(who are you?)
—afterwards everyone went off on his own, profiles.

I looked at the sky and the earth and straight ahead
and since then I've been writing a long letter to the dead
on a typewriter that doesn't have a ribbon, only a horizon line
so the words beat in vain and nothing stays.

I stand with my hand on the door handle, take the pulse of the
    house.

Väggarna är så fulla av liv
(barnen vågar inte sova ensamma uppe på kammarn—det som gör
mig trygg gör dem oroliga).

3 augusti. Där ute i det fuktiga gräset
hasar en hälsning från medeltiden: vinbergssnäckan
den subtilt grågulglimmande snigeln med sitt hus på svaj,
inplanterad av munkar som tyckte om *escargots*—ja
franciskanerna var här,
bröt sten och brände kalk, ön blev deras 1288, donation av kung
   Magnus
("Tessa almoso ok andra slika / the möta honom nw i
   hymmerike")
skogen föll, ugnarna brann, kalken seglades in
till klosterbyggena...
                    Syster snigel
står nästan stilla i gräset, känselspröten sugs in
och rullas ut, störningar och tveksamhet...
Vad den liknar mig själv i mitt sökande!

Vinden som blåst så noga hela dagen
—på de yttersta kobbarna är stråna allesammans räknade—
har lagt sig ner stilla inne på ön. Tändstickslågan står rak.
Marinmålningen och skogsmålningen mörknar tillsammans.
Också femvåningsträdens grönska blir svart.

The walls so full of life
(the children won't dare sleep alone up in the attic—what makes
    me feel safe makes them uneasy.)

August 3. Out there in the damp grass
slithers a greeting from the Middle Ages: Helix pomatia
the subtly gray-gold shining snail with its jaunty house,
introduced by some monks who liked *escargots*—yes, the
    Franciscans were here,
broke stone and burnt lime, the island was theirs in 1288, a
    donation from King Magnus
("Thes almes and othres he hath yeven / Thei meteth hym nu he
    entreth hevene.")
the forest fell, the ovens burned, the lime taken by sail
to the building of the monastery...
                         Sister snail
stands almost still in the grass, feelers sucked in
and rolled out, disturbances and hesitation...
How like myself in my searching!

The wind that blew so carefully all day—
all the blades of grass are counted on the furthest islets—
has laid down in the middle of the island. The matchstick's flame
    stands straight up.
The sea painting and the forest painting darken together.
Also the foliage of the five-story trees is turning black.

"Varje sommar är den sista". Det är tomma ord
för varelserna i sensommarmidnatten
där syrsorna syr på maskin som besatta
och Östersjön är nära
och den ensamma vattenkranen reser sig bland törnrosbuskarna
som en ryttarstaty. Vattnet smakar järn.

"Every summer is the last." These are empty words
for the creatures at late summer midnight
where the crickets sew on their machines as if possessed
and the Baltic's near
and the lonely water tap stands among the wild rose bushes
like an equestrian statue. The water tastes of iron.

VI

Mormors historia innan den glöms: hennes föräldrar dör unga,
fadern först. När änkan känner att sjukdomen ska ta också henne
går hon från hus till hus, seglar från ö till ö
med sin dotter. "Vem kan ta hand om Maria!" Ett främmande hus
på andra sidan fjärden tar emot. Där har de råd.
Men de som hade råd var inte de goda. Fromhetens mask spricker.
Marias barndom tar slut i förtid, hon går som piga utan lön
i en ständig köld. Många år. Den ständiga sjösjukan
under de långa rodderna, den högtidliga terrorn
vid bordet, minerna, gäddskinnet som knastrar
i munnen: var tacksam, var tacksam.

                                Hon såg sig aldrig tillbaka
men just därför kunde hon se Det Nya
och gripa tag i det.
Bort ur inringningen!

Jag minns henne. Jag tryckte mig mot henne
och i dödsögonblicket (övergångsögonblicket?) sände hon ut en
    tanke
så att jag—femåringen—förstod vad som hänt
en halvtimme innan de ringde.

My grandmother's story before it's forgotten: her parents dying
     young,
the father first. When the widow realizes the disease will take her
     too
she walks from house to house, sails from island to island
with her daughter. "Who can take care of Maria?"
A strange house on the other side of the bay takes her in.
They could afford to do it. But the ones that could afford it
     weren't the good ones.
Piety's mask cracks. Maria's childhood ends too soon,
she's an unpaid servant, in perpetual coldness.
Year after year. Perpetually seasick behind the
long oars, the solemn terror
at the table, the expressions, the pike skin crunching
in her mouth: be grateful, be grateful.
                                        She never looked back.
But because of this she could see The New
and seize it.
Break out of the bonds.

I remember her, I used to snuggle against her
and at the moment she died (the moment she passed over?) she
     sent out a thought
so that I, a five-year-old, understood what had happened
a half an hour before they called.

Jag minns henne. Med på nästa bruna foto
är den okände—
dateras enligt kläderna till förra seklets mitt.
En man omkring trettio: de kraftiga ögonbrynen,
ansiktet som ser mig rätt in i ögonen
och viskar: "här är jag".
Men vem "jag" är
finns det inte längre någon som minns. Ingen.

TBC? Isolering?

En gång stannade han
i den steniga gräsångande backen från sjön
och kände den svarta bindeln för ögonen.

Här, bakom täta snår—är det öns äldsta hus?
Den låga knuttimrade 200-åriga sjöboden med gråraggigt tungt
    trä.
Och det moderna mässingslåset har klickat igen om alltsammans,
    lyser som ringen i nosen på en gammal tjur
som vägrar att resa sig.
Så mycket hopkurat trä. På taket de uråldriga tegelpannorna som
    rasat kors och tvärs på varann
(det ursprungliga mönstret rubbat av jordens rotation genom
    åren)
det påminner om något...jag var där...vänta: det är den gamla

I remember her. But in the next brown photo
someone I don't know—
by the clothes from the middle of the last century.
A man about thirty, the powerful eyebrows,
the face that looks me right in the eye
whispering: "Here I am."
But who "I" am
is something no one remembers any more. No one.

TB? Isolation?

Once he stopped
on the stony, grass-streaming slope coming up from the sea
and felt the black blindfold in front of his eyes.

Here, behind the thick brush—is it the island's oldest house?
The low, knot-trimmed two-hundred-year-old fisherman's hut,
      with coarse, gray, heavy beams.
And the modern brass padlock has clicked together on all of it,
      shining like the ring in the nose of an old bull
that refuses to get up.
So much crouching wood. And on the roof the ancient tiles that
      collapsed across and on top of each other
(the original pattern erased by the earth's rotation through the
      years)
it reminds me of something...I was there...wait: it's the old Jewish

judiska kyrkogården i Prag
där de döda lever tätare än i livet, stenarna tätt tätt.
Så mycket inringad kärlek! Tegelpannorna med lavarnas
skrivtecken på ett okänt språk
är stenarna på skärgårdsfolkets ghettokyrkogård, stenarna
uppresta och hoprasade.—
Rucklet lyser
av alla dem som fördes av en viss våg, av en viss vind
hit ut till sina öden.

  cemetery in Prague

where the dead live closer together than they did in life, the stones
  jammed in, jammed in.

So much encircled love! The tiles with the lichen's letters in an
  unknown language

are the stones in the archipelago people's ghetto cemetery, the
  stones erected and fallen down—

The ramshackle hut shines

with the light of all the people carried by the certain wave, the
  certain wind,

out here to their fates.

AFTERWORD

On a sunny, hot summer day in 1972 two Swedish friends, the
poets Gunnar Harding and Gösta Friberg and their wives Lotta
Harding and Helene Brodin, walked up the gravel driveway
of the summer house my wife Annie and I were renting in the
forest outside of Stockholm. I'd asked if they could also invite
another poet I knew by name only, Tomas Tranströmer, and he
was there in the group with his wife Monica. Since it was to be an
afternoon of poetry and talk, for this one time all of our children
were left at home, except for our five-year-old daughter Mallay.
I still have the pictures Annie took of the afternoon, Tomas
curious and a little wary, in an open shirt, slacks, and sandals,
Monica more formally dressed in a skirt. Annie and I had been
in Sweden for a year and a half, but our grasp of the language
was still only tentative and the others mostly talked to each other
in their familiar Swedish. For the two younger poets Tomas
was already marked as the most promising writer Sweden had
produced in decades, and they were as respectful of him as I was,
though Tomas just laughed and shrugged off any pretensions.
Gunnar and Gösta were editors of a small poetry journal and
they intended to publish Tomas in forthcoming numbers.

I had no way of knowing it that afternoon, but Tomas and
Monica would become close friends, and when we meet forty
years later we still laugh, listen to music together, and talk as
much as is possible after Tomas's partial paralysis from a stroke.
I also had no idea that within a few weeks after our first meeting
I would begin—slowly and with some misgivings—to translate

Tomas's poetry. We had enough chances to talk together during that first afternoon to realize we wanted to talk more, so a few weeks later Annie and I drove west to the small city of Västerås where they were living. Annie took a few more pictures, and then when we went back to the house Tomas spread three or four books out on a table. He opened them to different English translations of one of his poems, and asked plaintively which one did I think was the best? For the next hour we sat picking over the translations, and we have continued to do it for as long as I've known him, even though his stroke makes it difficult now to go over specific words and phrases.

The summer house we'd rented was close to the road Tomas traveled when he drove to Stavsnäs harbor to take the ferry out to the small wood frame house on the island of Runmarö where he and his family spent every summer. Within a few months he began stopping by as he passed, and on these first visits he would bring with him sections of *Baltics* as he completed them, so I could start on the translation. I remember one afternoon when he called to say he had to hurry to Västerås, so could I meet him at the corner of our dirt road. When he drove up he smiled apologetically, rolled down the car window, and handed me a manuscript copy of the fifth section of the poem, the lines beginning,

> July 30.   The channel has become eccentric—today it's
> teeming with jellyfish for the first time in years...

In the spring of 1975 Annie and I, with two daughters now, Mallay and Nora, moved into a house that was one of a group of turn-of-the-century artists' villas closer to Stockholm. It was

Photo: Ann Charters

The first meeting with Tomas at our summer house in Eriksvik, east of Stockholm, in the summer of 1972. Left to right are Tomas Tranströmer, Monica Tranströmer, Gunnar Harding, Lotta Harding, Samuel Charters, Gösta Friberg, and Helene Brodin.

even easier for Tomas to stop on his drives between Runmarö and Västerås and we saw him often. It was a large house, built in 1905 by one of the young and talented Swedish artists who were studying together in Paris in the 1880s and then returned to Sweden to apply what they'd learned to depicting their Swedish forests and rocky coastlines. The house had a typically spacious upstairs studio which had an upright piano that had been there when the house was new. Tomas had quickly understood that like him I was also an enthusiastic amateur pianist, and we had already begun playing four hand duets on his piano in his living room in Västerås. We had a small repertoire of pieces composed for piano duet—two Mozart sonatas and a set of variations, some Brahms waltzes, and—our most ambitious number—the Schubert F-Minor Fantasy. We also tried any other music that turned up, and I remember one afternoon the two of us playing arrangements of Beethoven's symphonies for four hands—but this time playing them on a tiny clavichord that stood against another wall in the studio. The whispering sound of those massive Beethoven chords on the delicately toned little instrument was so incongruous that we finally began laughing too hard to continue.

Through all of these years, on our visits to Västerås or Runmarö or Tomas's visits to the house, on our meetings in Stockholm with Tomas and Monica, on the days when they visited us in Connecticut or I met them in hotels in Pittsburgh, or Washington, D.C. or in Cambridge, Massachusetts—it was taken for granted that I would continue translating all of his new poems. I also went back to his earlier collections and we worked on those poems together. I had no connection to literary journals in England or the United States, so once Tomas and I had managed to work through all the problems and I had finished

Photo: Lotta Harding

Tranströmer and Charters performing the Schubert F-Minor Fantasy for a summer crawfish party at the apartment of Gunnar and Lotta Harding in 1976. As Tomas wrote in "Schubertiana":

> *We crowd up to the piano and play with four hands in*
> *F-minor, two drivers for the same carriage, it looks*
> *a little ridiculous.*

It was the only time we ever played for anyone except our wives, who usually were busy doing other things at the same time. It was Annie who told us once, "This music is so heroic." Perhaps because of the loose, informal summer mood of the party or because we'd both drunk considerable aquavit it's the only time I remember that we made it through the whole Fantasy without having to stop to find out where we were.

Photo: Ann Charters

Tomas visiting the Charters, summer 1972

a new translation I sent him a copy to do with as he pleased. As his writing continued to move in new directions, to take on new breadths as his rich metaphors opened the poetry to ever more startling perceptions, I often found myself calling him in Västerås to tell him how much the new poem he'd just sent had moved me. Sometimes he or Monica would call unexpectedly—someone in Australia needed a new poem translated for a magazine, could I do the poem for them? Before Tomas's reading tours in the United States I often did translations for him, which would be in American English, and we could go over pronunciations for his American audiences. There were two nights at the Folger Library in Washington, D.C., where we shared the program as The Poet and his Translator.

I learned quickly that sitting with Tomas and working on one of his poems with him could be a challenging process. His English was very good, and it was important to him that the linguistic irregularities in many of the Swedish poems should also be there in the English versions. Protesting that this would make people feel that I didn't know what I was doing made no impression at all, and we wrangled continuously—though always good naturedly—over whether the translation was still solely a Tranströmer poem, or did I have any say in the final version. I sometimes envied the translators who were bringing his poetry over into languages he couldn't speak, since the expected translator's struggles wouldn't present so many challenges. Tomas responded to our years of working together by translating a lengthy narrative prose poem of mine for publication in a Swedish literary journal.

Though Monica and I had talked several times in the weeks before Tomas was afflicted and she told me she was worried that he seemed to be having some problem with his health, I still was stunned when she called me to say that he had suffered a stroke. I was aware that the poems I had been reading for the last few months had become darker in mood and she had said he was suffering from depression and was taking medication for the symptoms. When I went to the hospital it still seemed that the effects of the stroke would only be temporary. As he stood shakily beside his bed he looked almost embarrassed that he was causing everyone so much worry, though he could say only a few words and his right leg, arm, and hand were paralyzed. There was no way we could have known that he would never regain much more than only limited speech and movement. One night as Monica and I were walking back to the apartment she had borrowed through an acquaintance in Stockholm's Old Town while Tomas was in the hospital she began talking about the uncertain future. She said over and over that she didn't know if her shoulders would be strong enough for the burden she realized she might soon be bearing.

It became clear, after the cruel disappointment of months of therapy that made only a limited improvement on Tomas's condition, that Monica's shoulders were strong enough to give support to Tomas as well as to their daughters and eventually to their granddaughter. For the decades since the stroke she has made it possible for him to continue his literary life, to travel to accept new literary awards, and she has welcomed the steady stream of young writers, literary scholars, and translators who find their way to the house on Runmarö or to their apartment in Stockholm. When we meet again for lunch at the apartment, or for a chance once more to attend a concert together there are often moments of the same laughter, the same interest in what is happening with other writers and musicians, the familiar talk about our daughters, and about mutual friends in Sweden and the United States that we have known for years.

It is Monica now who must talk for Tomas, but it feels sometimes as though we're back again in the kitchen in Runmarö and soon he will lead us off into the forest that stretches behind their old channel pilot's cottage. He'll take us along faint grassy paths that he has known about since he was a boy growing up on the island, hurrying into the forest to search for mushrooms. He'll stop for a moment to tell us to listen to the sounds of the birds or to the high-pitched whine of the crickets, and often his destination will be a rocky slope in the warm sun for us to sit and look out at the sea. I know sadly that it won't happen, but I have some consolation in the knowledge that for everyone who loves his poetry those moments will be there always in the vibrant, etched lines and the questing images of his poems.

SAMUEL CHARTERS
Storrs
2011

RUNMARÖ AUGUST 1973

A PHOTO ESSAY BY ANN CHARTERS

The harbor

. . . on the stony, grass-streaming slope coming up from the sea.

from "Baltics"

On the walk to the Tranströmer house

The path to the Tranströmer house

. . . *I stand in the dense forest and look toward the house with its haze-blue walls. As if I had recently died and saw the house from a new angle.*

It has stood more than eighty summers. Its wood is impregnated with four times joy and three times sorrow. When someone who lived in the house dies it is repainted. The dead person himself does the painting, without a brush, from within . . .

from "The Blue House"

The kitchen in the stuga

The bedroom in the stuga

My grandmother's story before it's forgotten: her parents dying young,
the father first.

from "Baltics"

Tomas's harmonium

The mailboxes for the Tranströmers and their neighbors

A meadow fence

A path to the forest

Monica Tranströmer

Tomas and Monica walk in the forest,
where Tomas gathers mushrooms

The wind walks in the pine forest. It sighs heavily, lightly.
In the middle of the forest the Baltic also sighs, deep in the forest
you're out on the open sea.

from "Baltics"

In the middle of the forest there's an unexpected clearing that can only be found by those who have lost their way.

The clearing is encircled by a forest that's choking itself. Black trunks with ash gray stubble of lichens. Trees dead all the way up to the top, where some solitary still-growing branches touch the light. Underneath shadow that broods on shadow, the growing swamp.

But in the open space the grass is wonderfully green and alive. There are some larger stones there, arranged as if in a pattern. They must be the foundations for a house, maybe I'm wrong. Who lived here? No one can give any information about it, the name's somewhere in an archive no one opens (it's only the archives that stay young). The oral tradition is dead. Gypsy tribes remember, but people who can read and write forget. Make a note and forget . . .

from "The Clearing"

A fisherman's boathouse near the coast

And now: the stretch of open water, without doors, the open
    boundaries
that grow broader and broader
the further you stretch out.

from "Baltics"

Fishing nets

On the coast of Runmarö

Tomas and Uncle Elof

Tomas on the landing dock

Here, behind the thick brush—is it the island's oldest house?
The low, knot-trimmed two-hundred-year-old fisherman's hut
with coarse, gray, heavy beams.

from "Baltics"

. . . the modern brass padlock has clicked together on all of it,
    shining like the ring in the nose of an old bull
that refuses to get up.

from "Baltics"

. . . And on the roof the ancient tiles that
collapsed across and on top of each other.

from "Baltics"

Tomas on Runmarö

PHOTOGRAPHING TRANSTRÖMER

". . . my poems always have a definite geographical starting point."

—Tomas Tranströmer, from an interview with Gunnar Harding

In August 1973 I photographed Tomas and Monica Tranströmer at their summer home on the island of Runmarö in the Stockholm archipelago. My poet friends Gunnar Harding and Gösta Friberg had asked me to photograph Tomas on the island. They wanted to illustrate a section of *Baltics* that was scheduled to appear in *Lyrikvännen*, the Swedish literary magazine they edited in Stockholm, before the entire poem was published in the fall of 1974. I brought along my Rollieflex and Nikon cameras, the same cameras I'd used to photograph Jack Kerouac in Hyannis and Charles Olson in Gloucester several years earlier.

I also had a personal reason to photograph Tomas and Monica. I had known them for over a year and I was fascinated by the way that the two of them seemed extraordinarily connected. What I felt in their company during the days I spent on Runmarö was that the island was an idyllic summer paradise, an earthly Eden. Its unspoiled nature and its casual offering of total privacy made it the perfect setting for a photo essay about *Baltics* and the Tranströmers. Here I could create images that suggested what I saw as the ground of Tomas's poetry. His responses to his experience are firmly rooted in his intensely private family life. They are manifested in the people and the landscape he loves in the archipelago where his grandfather had been a ship's pilot.

I began my essay with photographs suggesting the walk to the Tranströmers' house from the jetty, after the boat from

Photo: Samuel Charters

Tomas Tranströmer, Monica Tranströmer, Gunnar Harding, Lotta Harding, Gösta Friberg, Helene Brodin, Ann Charters, 1972

Stavsnäs harbor had docked on the short trip to Runmarö and then moved on. Tomas was waiting for me, but we were too busy talking for me to use my cameras. I returned to the pier a day or so later to photograph the twenty-minute walk that put distance between the Baltic Sea and Tomas's small house located further inland. It was grouped along a meandering dirt road that joined his neighbors. He told me that his house was always painted light blue and had belonged to his mother and grandparents. Later I smiled to see that he hadn't exaggerated when he said it looked "like a child's drawing" in his poem "The Blue House."

I slept in the guesthouse or "stuga" across the path to the blue house, where the Transtömers lived with their two young daughters Emma and Paula. Most of my interior photos were taken in the stuga, where the light seemed to cooperate with the mood I was trying to capture.

Sam had stayed at home in Stockholm with our daughters Mallay and Nora, so I came alone to Runmarö. I took several long rambling walks throughout the island with Tomas and Monica. On one of our walks he pointed out the massive pile of rocks that he would describe in "The Clearing."

On another walk I stayed behind on the path to photograph Tomas and Monica together in the forest. He carried a plastic bag to hold the mushrooms he was picking. She sautéed them that evening to make a delicious first course for our dinner. I think that the sequence of photographs I took of them walking and talking together surrounded by the dense, silent forest suggests their vital companionship. Also, as Sam wrote in his introduction to *Baltics*, the different sections of the poem itself somehow give the impression of "taking a summer walk with Tomas across the island's stretches of forest and overgrown fields."

On another day Tomas rowed a small boat owned by his uncle, Elof Westerberg, who wanted to go fishing. I followed along and took photographs. I became fascinated by the weathered surfaces of the buildings near the coast. I felt that they were dramatic equivalents of the seascape evoked in *Baltics*. Perhaps it was because I became so immersed in the harshly stunning details of the individual boards and roof tiles that later when I turned to Tomas, I posed him against the clear, empty sky. These are my favorite portraits of Tranströmer. One was used on the cover of an early American edition of his poetry. It also illustrated Sam's translation of Tomas's poem "Övergångsstället, The Crosswalk," on a large Portents broadside that we published in the 1980s.

ANN CHARTERS
Storrs
2011

ABOUT THE AUTHOR

Tomas Tranströmer, winner of the 2011 Nobel Prize in Literature, is one of the most celebrated and influential poetic figures of his generation. He was born in Stockholm in 1931 and educated at Södra Latin School and the University of Stockholm, where he received a degree in psychology. He began his psychology career in the early 1960s at Roxtuna, a juvenile corrections institute in Sweden, and worked for several decades in the field. Since the publication of *17 Dikter* (*17 Poems*) in 1954, Tranströmer has written eleven full-length collections of poetry, most recently *Den stora gåtan* (*The Vast Enigma*) in 2004. He is one of the world's most translated poets, with books appearing in numerous editions in over fifty languages. In addition to his renown as a poet, Tranströmer is also a highly regarded amateur pianist and entomologist. He lives with his wife in Stockholm.

ABOUT THE TRANSLATOR

In 1972, a year after moving to Sweden with his wife Ann and their four-year-old daughter, Samuel Charters met Tomas Tranströmer and began translating his poetry. It was the beginning of a lifelong friendship and of many hours spent with Tranströmer's luminous writing. Charters soon began translating other Swedish poets, publishing works by, among others, Kjell Espmark, Gösta Friberg, Rolf Aggestam, and Wilhelm Eklund. He was awarded an Artur Lundquist translation stipendium and also a translation grant from the Finnish government. He traveled often to Finland to became more familiar with the work of the writers from the Swedish population still present in Finland today, and translated the poetry of Henry Parland, Elmer Diktonius, Rabbe Enckell, and Gunnar Björling. His translation of the incisive poems of Finland Swedish writer Edith Södergran, *We Women*, was the first collection of her writing to be published in English. He also published a translation of Bo Carpelan's *The Courtyard*, a collection of autobiographical poems describing Carpelan's childhood in Helsingfors (Helsinki). Charters' most recent translations are a selection in rhymed verse of poems from *Tales of Second Lieutenant Stoll* by Johan Ludvig Runeberg, and an expanded edition of Edith Södergran's *We Women*, which is forthcoming with Tavern Books.

ABOUT THE PHOTOGRAPHER

Ann Charters is the author of the first biography of Jack Kerouac in 1973 as well as a number of major studies of Beat literature and its personalities. She began taking photographs in 1958 on Andros Island in the Bahamas to document Samuel Charters' field recordings for Folkways Records. Their photographs of musicians are featured in *Blues Faces: A Portrait of the Blues* (David Godine Books, 2000). Her photographs of Kerouac, Ginsberg, Kesey and others are included in *Beats & Company: Portrait of a Literary Generation* (Doubleday, 1986). Her photo essay on Charles Olson in Gloucester was published in *Olson/Melville: A Study in Affinity* (Oyez, 1968). Her photos also illustrated Samuel Charters' *The Poetry of the Blues* (Oak Publications, 1963).

ABOUT TAVERN BOOKS

Tavern Books is a not-for-profit organization that exists to print, promote, and preserve works of literary vision, to foster a climate of cultural preservation, and to disseminate books in a way that benefits the reading public. In addition to reviving out-of-print books, we publish works in translation from the world's finest poets. We keep our titles in print, honoring the cultural contract between publisher and author, as well as between publisher and public. Our catalog, known as The Living Library, sustains the visions of our authors, ensuring their voices are alive in the social and artistic discourse of our modern era.

THE LIVING LIBRARY

Casual Ties by David Wevill

The Boy Changed into a Stag Clamors at the Gate of Secrets
by Ferenc Juhász,
translated from the Hungarian by David Wevill

Under an Arkansas Sky by Jo McDougall

Arthur's Talk with the Eagle by Anonymous,
translated from the Welsh by Gwyneth Lewis

Twelve Poems about Cavafy by Yannis Ritsos,
translated from the Greek by Paul Merchant

Night of Shooting Stars by Leonardo Sinisgalli,
translated from the Italian by W. S. Di Piero

Prodigy by Charles Simic,
drawings by Charles Seluzicki

Ocean by Joseph Millar

The Countries We Live In by Natan Zach,
translated from the Hebrew by Peter Everwine

Notes on Sea & Shore by Greta Wrolstad

Buson: Haiku by Yosa Buson,
translated from the Japanese by Franz Wright

Ashulia by Zubair Ahmed

Archeology by Adrian C. Louis

Prison by Tomas Tranströmer
with a postscript by Jonas Ellerström,
translated from the Swedish by Malena Mörling

Tomas Tranströmer's First Poems and *Notes From the Land of Lap Fever*
by Tomas Tranströmer and with a commentary by Jonas Ellerström,
translated from the Swedish by Malena Mörling

Six-Minute Poems: The Last Poems by George Hitchcock

Baltics by Tomas Tranströmer
with photographs by Ann Charters,
translated from the Swedish by Samuel Charters

For the Living and the Dead by Tomas Tranströmer,
translated from the Swedish by John F. Deane

My Blue Piano by Else Lasker-Schüler,
translated from the German by Eavan Boland

Collected Poems: Volume One by David Wevill

The Wounded Alphabet: Collected Poems 1963-1983
by George Hitchcock

Glowing Enigmas by Nelly Sachs,
translated from the German by Michael Hamburger

Who Whispered Near Me by Killarney Clary

The Fire's Journey: Volume One by Eunice Odio,
translated from the Spanish by Keith Ekiss
with Sonia P. Ticas and Mauricio Espinoza

Selected Poems by Ferenc Juhász,
translated from the Hungarian by David Wevill

Fire Water World and *Among the Dog Eaters*
by Adrian C. Louis

We Women by Edith Södergran,
translated from the Swedish by Samuel Charters

Collected Poems: Volume Two by David Wevill

Winterward by William Stafford

The Wounded Alphabet: Collected Poems 1984-2010
by George Hitchcock

The End of Space by Albert Goldbarth

COLOPHON

This book was designed and typeset by Michael McGriff. The text is set in Garamond, an old-style serif typeface named for the punch-cutter Claude Garamond (c. 1480 – 1561). The cover, titles, and front matter are set in Garamond and Myriad, a humanist sans-serif typeface designed by Robert Slimbach and Carol Twombly. Printed on archival-quality paper at McNaughton & Gunn, Inc.

In this edition, twenty-six copies have been bound into boards and are signed and lettered A – Z by the translator and photographer.